# HISTORY OF THE BREED

Scotland has laid claim to five terriers: Skye, Cairn, Scottie, Dandie Dinmont and the West Highland White. Like the chicken or the egg there is constant debate over which came first, and which breed was developed from the other. As one dog historian has pointed out, Scotland is a mountainous country, its dogmen a stay-at-home lot; consequently each clan bred its terriers according to its own ideas.

A great many historians, however, seem to think that the Skye is the oldest of all five breeds (but not as we know it today) and that the West Highland White, or Westie as he is commonly called, is the Johnny-come-lately. He was recognized in England by The Kennel Club as a separate breed in 1907, and by the American Kennel Club in 1909.

How the Skye Terrier got to Scotland no one knows, but there is a wonderful legend that a

The West Highland White Terrier was recognized in England in 1907 and by the American Kennel Club in 1909. It is a hugely popular breed.

Maltese and a Poodle were shipwrecked on the Isle of Skye off the northern coast of Scotland when the Spanish Armada met its doom, and that all the terriers from Scotland are their descendants. This happened during Queen Elizabeth's reign. Legend it may be, but it is a matter of record that her successor, James I, wrote to Edinburgh to ask that half a dozen "earth dogges or Terrieres" from Argyllshire be sent to France as a present; not only that, he also directed they be sent on two or more ships for fear of shipwreck, so he must have realized their rarity and worth.

The name "Terrier" comes from the Latin word *terra*, which means earth, and it is for this reason all these breeds were, in the old days, called "earth dogs" because when chasing prey they burrowed deep into their holes, an expression known to hunters as "going to earth."

The Westie was bred in solid white, or almost so, because one was killed when mistaken for a rabbit! At least that's the story passed on from Scotland.

In the 19th century the Westie was known as the Pittenweem, Roseneath or Poltalloch Terrier. Sir Edward Landseer pictured one in his portrait of two dogs, Dignity and Impudence, painted in 1839. "Dignity" is a Bloodhound, "Impudence" quite obviously a West Highland White.

Roseneath was the estate name of the Duke of Argyll, from whom James I had requested the "earth dogges," and Poltalloch, the home of the Malcolm family, who were also early breeders. The Malcolm family, in fact, is usually credited with originating the West Highland White, then known, derisively, as a "White Cairn." In those days there seems to have been a superstitious prejudice against "White Cairns" and when one turned up in a litter it was destroyed.

The Malcolms felt otherwise. While shooting with his hunting pack of small terriers, Colonel E.D. Malcolm, killed one of his dark-colored dogs,

The Malcolm family is generally credited with originating the Westie breed. They originally were disparagingly called *White Cairn Terriers* and when a white pup showed up in a Cairn litter, it was destroyed!

thinking it was a rabbit. This disturbed him so much that he swore he would breed only light colored dogs from then on. He bred for a white (or near white) hunter of small stature, great courage and high determination, with a fine double coat to protect him against the teeth of the rat and other vermin as well as the brutal northern climate. What he came up with was the West Highland White pretty much as we know him today. As one Westie lover has pointed out: "No water was ever too cold and no earth ever too deep for them."

The Westie's show career has been relatively short when compared with many other breeds, as the first West Highland White was not shown in the United States until 1906. This was at the Westminster Kennel Club Show in New York City under the classification of "Roseneath Terriers."

Westies are small, well-balanced and hardy. They are proud, even arrogant dogs, well built with a deep chest and a straight back. Their powerful hindquarters and muscular legs enable them to sit in this position for quite a while.

# STANDARD FOR THE BREED

A breed standard is the criterion by which the appearance (and to a certain extent, the temperament as well) of any given dog is made subject to objective measurement. Basically, the standard for any breed is a definition of the perfect dog, to which all specimens of the breed are compared. Breed standards are always subject to change through review by the national breed club for each dog, so it is always wise to keep up with developments in a breed by checking the publications of your national kennel club.

A lot of hair should be left on the Westie's head to act as a frame for the typical, attractive Westie expression. The coat should be about two inches long.

## STANDARD FOR THE WEST HIGHLAND WHITE TERRIER

**General Appearance**—The West Highland White Terrier is a small, game, well-balanced, hardy looking terrier, exhibiting good showmanship, possessed with no small amount of self-esteem, strongly built, deep in chest and back ribs, with a straight back and powerful hindquarters on muscular legs, and exhibiting in marked degree a great combination of strength and activity. The coat is about two inches long, white in color, hard, with plenty of soft undercoat. The dog should be neatly presented, the longer coat on the back and sides trimmed to blend into the shorter neck and shoulder coat. Considerable hair is left around the head to act as a frame for the face to yield a typical Westie expression.

**Size, Proportion, Substance**—The ideal size is 11 inches at the withers for dogs and ten for bitches. A slight deviation is accepted. The Westie is a compact dog, with good balance and substance. The body between the withers and the root of the tail is slightly shorter than the height at the withers. Short-coupled and well boned. *Faults*—Over or under height limits. Fine boned.

**Head**—Shaped to present a round appearance from the front. Should be in proportion to the body. *Expression*—Piercing, inquisitive, pert. *Eyes*—Widely set apart, medium in size, almond shaped, dark brown in color, deep set, sharp and intelligent. Looking from under heavy eyebrows, they give a piercing look. Eye rims are black. *Faults*—Small, full or light colored eyes. *Ears*—Small, carried tightly erect, set wide apart, on top outer edge of the skull. They terminate in a sharp point, and must never be cropped. The hair on the ears is trimmed short and is smooth and velvety, free of fringe at the tips. Black skin pigmentation is preferred. *Faults*—Round-pointed, broad, large ears set closely together, not held tightly erect, or placed too low on the side of the head. *Skull*—Broad, slightly longer than the muzzle, not flat on top but slightly domed between the ears. It gradually tapers to the eyes. There is a defined stop, eyebrows are heavy. *Faults*—Long or narrow skull. *Muzzle*—Blunt, slightly shorter than skull, powerful and gradually tapering to the nose which is large and

The typical Westie expression is described in the standard as *piercing, inquisitive, pert*. The eyes are widely set apart, medium in size, almond shaped and dark brown in color.

black. The jaws are level and powerful. Lip pigmentation is black. *Faults*—Muzzle longer than skull. Nose color other than black. *Bite*—The teeth are large for the size of the dog. There must be six incisor teeth between the canines of both upper and lower jaws. An occasional missing premolar is acceptable. *Faults*—Teeth defective or misaligned. Any incisors missing or seven premolars missing. Teeth overshot or undershot.

**Neck, Topline, Body—** *Neck*—Muscular and well set on sloping shoulders. The length of neck should be in proportion to the remainder of the dog. *Faults*—Neck too long or two short. *Topline*—Flat and level, both standing and moving. *Faults*—High rear, any deviation from above. *Body*—Compact and of good substance. Ribs deep and well arched in the upper half of rib, extending at least to the elbows, and

**EARS**
Small, erect, wide apart with sharp points.

**SKULL**
Broad, longer than muzzle, domed, not flat, tapers to the eyes.

**EYES**
Widely set apart, deep set, intelligent looking from under heavy eye brows, eye rims are black.

**HAIR**
White, 2 inches long, hard with lots of soft undercoat.

**BITE**
Large teeth, 6 incisors between the canines, top and bottom.

**NOSE**
Large, intensely black without any other marks. Nose color other than black is a disqualification.

**MUZZLE**
Blunt, shorter than skull, powerful and gradually tapering to the nose. Jaws are level and powerful.

**EXPRESSION**
Considered his main attribute. Piercing, pert and inquisitive. The standard does not call for it, but it should be beautiful and cute.

**TAIL**
Relatively short, with good substance and shaped like a carrot.

**COAT**
Very important and rarely seen to perfection. Double-coated. Head shaped by plucking hair. Outer coat straight, hard, white hair, long. Shorter on neck and shoulders.

**HINDQUARTERS**
Thighs are very muscular, well angulated, not set wide apart.

**LEGS**
Rear legs are short and muscled.

**HIND FEET**
Smaller than front feet and thickly padded. Dew claws may be removed.

**BODY**
Compact and of good substance. Ribs deep and well arched in the upper half.

**HEAD**
Shaped to present a round appearance from the front view. Should be in proportion to the body.

**NECK**
Muscular, well set on sloping shoulders. The length should be in proportion to the remainder of the dog.

**SKULL**
Broad, slightly longer than the muzzle, it gradually tapers to the eyes.

**TEETH**
Large for the size of dog. Six incisor teeth in both upper and lower jaws.

**FORELEGS**
Muscular and well boned, short but long enough so the dog is not too close to the ground.

**FOREFEET**
Larger than hind feet. Round and proportionate in size, strong, thickly padded. Can turn out slightly. Black pads.

straight, and thickly covered with short, hard hair. They are set in under the shoulder blades with definite body overhang before them. Height from elbow to withers and elbow to ground should be approximately the same. *Faults*—Out at elbows, light bone, fiddle-front. *Feet*—Forefeet are larger than the hind ones, are round, proportionate in size, strong, thickly padded; they may properly be turned out slightly. Dewclaws may be removed. Black pigmentation is

**The back should be straight and level and not drop from back to front.**

most desirable on pads of all feet and nails, although nails may lose coloration in older dogs.

**Hindquarters**— *Angulation*—Thighs are very muscular, well angulated, not set wide apart, with hock well bent, short and parallel when viewed from the rear. *Legs*—Rear legs are muscular and relatively short and sinewy. *Faults*—Weak hocks, long hocks, lack of angulation. Cowhocks. *Feet*—Hind feet are smaller than front feet, and are thickly padded. Dewclaws may be removed.

**Coat**—Very important and seldom seen to perfection. Must be double-coated. The head is shaped by plucking the hair, to present the round appearance. The outer coat consists of straight, hard, white hair, about two inches long, with shorter coat on neck and shoulders, properly blended and trimmed to blend shorter areas into furnishings, which are longer on stomach and legs. The ideal coat is hard, straight and white, but a hard straight coat which may have some wheaten tipping is preferable to a white, fluffy, or soft coat. *Faults*—Soft coat. Any silkiness or tendency to curl. Any open or single coat, or one which is too short.

**Color**—The color is white, as defined by the breed's name. *Faults*—Any coat color other than white. Heavy wheaten color.

**Gait**—Free, straight and easy all around. It is a distinctive gait, not stilted, but powerful, with reach and drive. In front the leg is freely extended forward by the shoulder. When seen from the front the legs do not move square, but tend to move toward the center of gravity. The hind movement is free, strong and fairly close. The hocks are freely flexed and drawn close under the body, so that when moving off the foot the body is thrown or pushed forward with some force. Overall ability to move is usually best evaluated from the side, and topline remains level. *Faults*—Lack of reach in front, and/or drive behind. Stiff, stilted or too wide movement.

**Temperament**—Alert, gay, courageous and self-reliant, but friendly. *Faults*—Excess timidity or excess pugnacity.

Taking away a hazardous vinyl toy should not be a dangerous experience. The Westie should not growl or bite when its mistress removes the dangerous toy.

When Westies are young their ears may drop and they may not show their true conformation to the breed standard. If you want a show dog, bring along an expert to help you make your selection.

note on whether or not the puppy has been wormed; a diet and feeding schedule to which the puppy is accustomed) and you are welcomed as a fellow owner to a long, pleasant association with a most lovable pet, and more (news)paper work.

### GENERAL PREPARATION

You have chosen to own a particular Westie puppy. You have chosen it very carefully over all other breeds and all other puppies. So before you ever get that Westie puppy home, you will have prepared for its arrival by reading everything you can get your hands on having to do with the management of Westies and puppies. True, you will run into many conflicting opinions, but at least you will not be starting "blind." Read, study, digest. Talk over your plans with your veterinarian, other "Westie people," and the seller of your Westie puppy.

When you get your Westie puppy, you will find that your reading and study are far from finished. You've just scratched the surface in your plan to provide the greatest possible comfort and health for your Westie; and, by the same token, you do want to assure yourself of the greatest possible enjoyment of this wonderful creature. You must be ready for this puppy mentally as

People who love Westies are seldom satisfied with one specimen. Breeders often keep a number of dogs and bitches for the sake of seeking perfect matches.

If you are lucky enough to find a well trained older Westie, don't hesitate to buy it. They are quick to adapt to a new home and new owners. Westies are very intelligent. Whoever feeds and cares for them owns their heart.

well as in the physical requirements.

### TRANSPORTATION

If you take the puppy home by car, protect him from drafts, particularly in cold weather. Wrapped in a towel and carried in the arms or lap of a passenger, the Westie puppy will usually make the trip without mishap. If the pup starts to drool and to squirm, stop the car for a few minutes. Have newspapers handy in case of car-sickness. A covered carton lined with newspapers provides protection for puppy and car, if you are driving alone. Avoid excitement and unnecessary handling of the puppy on arrival.

A Westie puppy is a very small "package" to be making a complete change of surroundings and company, and he needs frequent rest and refreshment to renew his vitality.

### THE FIRST DAY AND NIGHT

When your Westie puppy arrives in your home, put him down on the floor and don't pick him up again, except when it is absolutely necessary. He is a dog, a real dog, and must not be lugged around like a rag doll. Handle him as little as possible, and permit no one to pick him up and baby him. To repeat, *put your Westie puppy on the floor or the ground and let him stay there except when it may be necessary to do otherwise.*

Quite possibly your Westie puppy will be afraid for a while in his new surroundings, without his mother and littermates. Comfort him and reassure him, but don't console him. Don't give him the "oh-you-poor-itsy-bitsy-puppy" treatment. Be calm, friendly, and reassuring. Encourage him to walk around and sniff over his new home. If it's dark, put on the lights. Let him roam for a few minutes while you and everyone else concerned sit quietly or go about your routine business. Let the puppy come back to you.

Playmates may cause an immediate problem if the new Westie puppy is to be greeted by children or other pets. If not, you can skip this subject.

The natural affinity between puppies and children calls for some supervision until a live-and-let-live relationship is established. This applies particularly to a Christmas puppy, when there is more excitement than usual and more chance for a puppy to swallow something upsetting. It is a better plan to welcome the puppy several days before or after the holiday week. Like a baby, your Westie puppy needs much rest and should not be over-handled. Once a child realizes that a puppy has "feelings" similar to his own, and can readily be hurt or injured, the opportunities for play and responsibilities provide exercise and training for both.

For his first night with you, he should be put where he is to

Let your puppy roam around your house getting acquainted with sights and smells. It will soon be looking for you.

If you buy two puppies it will be easier when you first bring them home since a lone puppy misses his mother and siblings and might spend the first night whining.

sleep every night—say in the kitchen, since its floor can usually be easily cleaned. Let him explore the kitchen to his heart's content; close doors to confine him there. Prepare his food and feed him lightly the first night. Give him a pan with some water in it—not a lot, since most puppies will try to drink the whole pan dry. Give him an old coat or shirt to lie on. Since a coat or shirt will be strong in human scent, he will pick it out to lie on, thus furthering his feeling of security in the room where he has just been fed.

## HOUSEBREAKING HELPS

Now, sooner or later—mostly sooner—your new Westie puppy is going to "puddle" on the floor. First take a newspaper and lay it on the puddle until the urine is soaked up onto the paper. *Save this paper.* Now take a cloth with soap and water, wipe up the floor and dry it well. Then take the wet paper and place it on a fairly large square of newspapers in a convenient corner. When cleaning up, always keep a piece of wet paper on top of the others. Every time he wants to "squat," he will seek out this spot and use the papers. (This routine is rarely necessary for more than three days.) Now leave your Westie puppy for the night. Quite probably he will cry and howl a bit; some are more stubborn than others on this matter. But let him stay alone for the night. This may seem harsh treatment, but it is the best procedure in the long run. Just let him cry; he will weary of it sooner or later.

During the puppy's explorations, don't let him get into trouble. Be sure your house is puppy-proof as a new Westie will investigate every place he can reach.

If your Westie gets hungry he might well attack the fruit bowl! Offer food on a regular schedule.

# FEEDING YOUR WESTIE

Now let's talk about feeding your Westie, a subject so simple that it's amazing there is so much nonsense and misunderstanding about it. Is it expensive to feed a Westie? No, it is not! You can feed your Westie economically and keep him in perfect shape the year round, or you can feed him expensively. He'll thrive either way, and let's see why this is true.

First of all, remember a Westie is a dog. Dogs do not have a high degree of selectivity in their food, and unless you spoil them with great variety (and possibly turn them into poor, "picky" eaters) they will eat almost anything that they become accustomed to. Many dogs flatly refuse to eat nice, fresh beef. They pick around it and eat everything else. But meat—bah! Why? They aren't accustomed to it! They'd eat rabbit fast enough, but they refuse beef because they aren't used to it.

## VARIETY NOT NECESSARY

A good general rule of thumb is forget all human preferences and don't give a thought to variety. Choose the right diet for your Westie and feed it to him day after day, year after year, winter and summer. But what is the right diet?

Hundreds of thousands of dollars have been spent in canine nutrition research. The results are pretty conclusive, so you needn't go into a lot of experimenting with trials of this and that every other week. Research has proven just what your dog needs to eat and to keep healthy.

An ideal snack for the Westie puppy is the Chicken Chooz. This is a hard, molded bone of chicken and cheese. It exercises the puppies teeth, gums and jaws while it satisfies its appetite and need to chew. This is a VERY high quality product with a 70% protein content! Most other treats have a 25% protein content, the rest being filler.

## DOG FOOD

There are almost as many right diets as there are dog experts, but the basic diet most often recommended is one that consists of a dry food, either meal or kibble form. There are several of excellent quality, manufactured by reliable companies, research tested, and nationally advertised. They are inexpensive, highly satisfactory, and easily available in stores everywhere in containers of five to 50 pounds. Larger amounts cost less per pound, usually.

from alfalfa and soy beans, as well as some dried-milk product. Note the vitamin content carefully. See that they are all there in good proportions; and be especially certain that the food contains properly high levels of vitamins A and D, two of the most perishable and important ones. Note the B-complex level, but don't worry about carbohydrate and mineral levels. These substances are

If you come home with two puppies, get two feeding dishes, plus a water dish. They can share the water, but it must be changed daily.

If you have a choice of brands, it is usually safer to choose the better known one; but even so, carefully read the analysis on the package. Do not choose any food in which the protein level is less than 25 percent, and be sure that this protein comes from both animal and vegetable sources. The good dog foods have meat meal, fish meal, liver, and such, plus protein

plentiful and cheap and not likely to be lacking in a good brand.

The advice given for how to choose a dry food also applies to moist or canned types of dog foods, if you decide to feed one of these.

Having chosen a really good food, feed it to your Westie as the manufacturer directs. And once you've started, stick to it. Never change if you can possibly help it.

Treats made for dogs are sold in pet shops. Although not healthy if used to excess, such treats are great for training and fun for your Westie.

## ALL WESTIES NEED TO CHEW

Puppies and young Westies need something with resistance to chew on while their teeth and jaws are developing—for cutting the puppy teeth, to induce growth of the permanent teeth under the puppy teeth, to assist in getting rid of the puppy teeth at the proper time, to help the permanent teeth through the gums, to ensure normal jaw development, and to settle the permanent teeth solidly in the jaws.

The adult Westie's desire to chew stems from the instinct for tooth cleaning, gum massage, and jaw exercise—plus the need for an outlet for periodic doggie tensions.

This is why dogs, especially puppies and young dogs, will often destroy property worth hundreds of dollars when their chewing instinct is not diverted from their owner's possessions. And this is why you should provide your Westie with something to chew—something that has the necessary functional qualities, is

Nylabone/Gumabone® Pooch Pacifiers enable the Westie to slowly chew off the knobs while they clean their own teeth. The knobs develop elastic frays which act like a toothbrush. These pacifiers are extremely effective as detailed scientific studies have shown. Replace the bone when the knobs have worn down.

desirable from the Westie's viewpoint, and is safe for him.

It is very important that your Westie not be permitted to chew on anything he can break or on any indigestible thing from which he can bite sizable chunks. Sharp pieces, such as from a bone which can be broken by a dog, may pierce the intestinal wall and kill. Indigestible things that can be bitten off in chunks, such as from shoes or rubber or plastic toys, may cause an intestinal stoppage (if not regurgitated) and bring painful death, unless surgery is promptly performed.

Strong natural bones, such as 4- to 8-inch lengths of round shin bone from mature beef—either the kind you can get from a butcher or one of the variety available commercially in pet stores—may serve your Westie's teething needs if his mouth is large enough to handle them effectively. You may be tempted to give your Westie puppy a smaller bone and he may not be able to break it when you do, but puppies grow rapidly and the power of their jaws constantly increases until maturity. This means that a growing Westie may break one of the smaller bones at any time, swallow the pieces, and die painfully before you realize what is wrong.

All hard natural bones are very abrasive. If your Westie is an avid chewer, natural bones may wear away his teeth prematurely; hence, they then should be taken away from your dog when the teething purposes have been served. The badly worn, and usually painful, teeth of many mature dogs can be

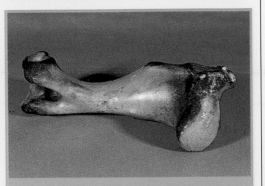

Pet shops sell real bones which have been colored, cooked, dyed or served natural. Some of these bones are huge and too large for Westies.

traced to excessive chewing on natural bones.

Contrary to popular belief, knuckle bones that can be chewed up and swallowed by your Westie provide little, if any, usable calcium or other nutriment. They do, however, disturb the digestion of most dogs and cause them to vomit the nourishing food they need.

Dried rawhide products of various types, shapes, sizes, and prices are available on the market

Westies must chew. There are special bones made just for puppies. They usually are filled with calcium supplements and are very hard. The most popular of the puppy bones is the one made by Nylabone®.

Contains real bone

PUPPY BONE.
POOCH PACIFIER

SAVES MONEY & DOGS' LIVES

For puppies with chewing and other behavioral problems

REGULAR SIZE

REGULAR SIZE

"WHY" On Reverse Side !

PUPPY BONE Pooch Pacifier®
NYLABONE CORP. P.O. Box 27 Neptune City, N.J. 07753

Rawhide is probably the most popular dog chew. It can be dangerous and cause a dog to choke on it as it swells when it gets wet. A better product is molded rawhide which is first melted and then molded. It doesn't swell when wet and it takes much longer to chew than plain rawhide. It is also much cleaner (its actually sterilized during the melting process!) and safer for your Westie.

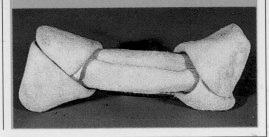

Most pet shops have complete walls dedicated to safe pacifiers.

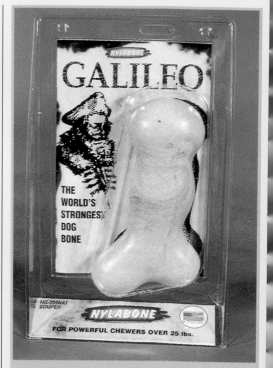

Some Westies are strong chewers and they require very strong chew devices. The Hercules is a dental device which is made from very heavy polyurethane and probably can't be destroyed by a Westie.

The Galileo is an extremely tough nylon pacifier. Its design is based upon original sketches by Galileo. A book explaining the history and workings of the design come inside each package. This might very well be the best design for a Westie.

Raised dental tips on each dog bone works wonders with controlling plaque in a Westie's teeth.

Get a medium size (regular) Nylabone for your Westie.

and have become quite popular. However, they don't serve the primary chewing functions very well; they are a bit messy when wet from mouthing, and most Westies chew them up rather rapidly—but they have been considered safe for dogs until recently. Now, more and more incidents of death, and near death, by strangulation have been reported to be the results of partially swallowed chunks of

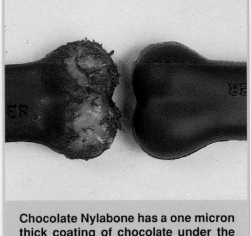

Chocolate Nylabone has a one micron thick coating of chocolate under the skin of the nylon. When the Westie chews it, the white sub-surface is exposed. This photo shows and before and after chewing.

A chicken-flavored Gumabone has tiny particles of chicken embedded in it to keep the Westie interested in chewing it. Westies can smell it, you can't. That's the way it should be!

rawhide swelling in the throat. More recently, some veterinarians have been attributing cases of acute constipation to large pieces of incompletely digested rawhide in the intestine.

A new product, molded rawhide, is very safe. During the process, the rawhide is melted and then injection molded into the familiar dog bone shape. It is very hard and is eagerly accepted by Westies. The melting process also sterilizes the rawhide. Don't confuse this with pressed rawhide, which is nothing more than small strips of rawhide squeezed together.

The nylon bones, especially those with natural meat and bone fractions added, are probably the most complete, safe, and economical answer to the chewing need. Dogs cannot break them or bite off sizable chunks; hence, they are completely safe—and being longer lasting than other things offered for the purpose, they are economical.

Pet shops sell dog treats which are healthy and nutritious. Cheese is added to chicken meal and other high protein foods to be melted together and molded into hard chew devices or pacifiers. Don't waste your money on low protein treats. If the pacifier doesn't have at least a 50% protein content, pass it up!

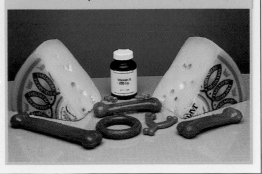

Don't use cheap, soft plastic squeak toys. Westies chew them apart and may swallow the indigestible chunks of plastic and get a fatal intestinal blockage. Some of the imported Oriental chew toys are hand painted with lead-containing colorings.

Hard chewing raises little bristle-like projections on the surface of the nylon bones—to provide effective interim tooth cleaning and vigorous gum massage, much in the same way your toothbrush does it for you. The little projections are raked off and swallowed in the form of thin shavings, but the chemistry of the nylon is such that they break down in the stomach fluids and pass through without effect.

The toughness of the nylon provides the strong chewing resistance needed for important jaw exercise and effectively aids teething functions, but there is no tooth wear because nylon is non-abrasive. Being inert, nylon does not support the growth of microorganisms; and it can be washed in soap and water or it can be sterilized by boiling or in an autoclave.

Nylabone® is highly recommended by veterinarians as a safe, healthy nylon bone that can't splinter or chip. Nylabone® is frizzled by the dog's chewing action, creating a toothbrush-like surface that cleanses the teeth and massages the gums. Nylabone®, the only chew products made of flavor-impregnated solid nylon, are available in your local pet shop. Nylabone® is superior to the cheaper bones because it is made of virgin nylon, which is the strongest and longest-lasting type of nylon available. The cheaper bones are made from recycled or re-ground nylon scraps, and have a tendency to break apart and split easily.

Nothing, however, substitutes for periodic professional attention for your Westie's teeth and gums, not any more than your toothbrush can do that for you. Have your Westie's teeth cleaned at least once a year by your veterinarian (twice a year is better) and he will be happier, healthier, and far more pleasant to live with.

Hard bones are better than soft bones for Westies. These Nylabones (one has already been chewed) have been proven safe for Westies over the last 40 years! They are absolutely guaranteed as to quality. Why take chances on inferior chews which are quickly destroyed because they are not made of virgin nylon?

You should be able to groom your Westie in your own home to look just like this one. Learn how to groom your Westie and do it on a regular basis.

# GROOMING YOUR WESTIE

## GENERAL GROOMING

Unlike other long-haired breeds, the Westie's coat is not difficult to keep in trim unless you are going to show him in the breed ring. In this case it would be advisable to have an expert groom him while you watch. Once you have your Westie trimmed, keep him groomed that way. However, if you plan to show don't wait until a week before to seek this help, as his coat may need considerable conditioning.

If you check the breed standard, you will see that your Westie should have a double coat consisting of a soft, thick undercoat with a hard outer coat, especially on the back and legs.

When you select your Westie, inquire about stripping the puppy coat as to give the new hard coat a chance to come in. If you do this when the dog is three months old or younger, his coat will be in good condition by the time he is six months old.

Your Westie is eligible to be shown in the puppy class when he is six months old. If there is a fun match, or sanctioned match, in your area, you would do well to attend.

Whether you plan to show your Westie or not, a daily brushing and combing is recommended, not only to promote the growth of his coat and keep him clean but also for his general health and well-being.

If friends or other members of the family groom him while he is young, he will not mind being handled or groomed later when you may wish to leave him in a kennel.

The Westie should be kept tidy. Beginning with the head, the ears should be pointed with all long hair on them removed by scissoring or with a stripping comb. The tips of the ears should look and feel like velvet. The hair on top of his head should not be longer than the ear tips. Tidy up the ruff around the face.

**Your local pet shop has special combs and brushes with which you can groom your Westie every day.**

Thin the hair under the neck, but do not remove chest hair except to tidy. The hair should be blended from the back of the neck and into the shoulder using a fine stripping comb. This not only removes dead hair in the coat but also enhances the beauty of your Westie.

The hair on the back and sides should be two inches long, and don't let anyone tell you otherwise.

As to the feet, keep claws well back and trim around the foot, removing hair between pads and toes. Use blunt-nosed scissors for this area. Remove all flying hair from the tail by plucking or stripping; then with scissors trim the hair on back of tail so as not to

What a gorgeous face! Well rounded and perfect in appearance. This can only be achieved by constant grooming of the face hairs to achieve the rounded appearance characteristic of the breed.

Groom your Westies regularly. Trying to demat an unkempt coat is hard work and not pleasant for the dog either.

Feed a great coat! Quality foods and a balanced diet will yield the best possible coat.

This is a professional groomer preparing to groom a Westie. Most professional groomers do a wonderful job on Westies. If you are too lazy or don't have the time, use a professional groomer in your neighborhood.

The dog after being groomed professionally looks like a different animal! You really should keep your Westie well groomed every day.

A wonderful chore for a child is to comb and brush the pet Westie. This develops a bond between the dog and the child while it teaches the child responsibility. The child is rewarded by the lovely appearance of the Westie.

flag; shape so the tail is pointed at the tip and somewhat broader at the base. It is best to trim before bathing, if a bath is necessary.

Trimming tools you will need are a metal comb, natural bristle brush (or one with plastic or rubber teeth), stripping comb (fine), blunt scissors, thinning shears, and claw clippers (or you may prefer a three-cornered file). An important thing to remember is to keep the claws trim (and this requires patience and practice) so as not to spoil the appearance of an otherwise good dog. He should be up on his toes when gaited, and this is impossible if the claws are neglected.

Plucking is not for beginners. It means pulling out the hairs by hand quickly and (almost) painlessly for the Westie. Grooming a Westie completely, toes included, is best left for the professional.

### BATHING

Westies require very little bathing and should not be bathed until more than six months old. Westies have dry skin and no offensive doggy odor. However, when it is necessary to bathe them, use a mild liquid detergent designed especially for dogs. It rinses away much better than soap. Care should be taken to prevent your dog from getting chilled after a bath, and he should be dry before he's allowed outdoors.

Take the time to place a drop of mineral oil or castor oil in each eye to protect them from the soap or detergent. This way your Westie won't have the unpleasant experience of soap burning in his eyes.

Look at the outside of your dog's ears, which should be cleaned carefully and thoroughly dried. Take special care that the water does not get inside of the ears. Once the ears are dried, put a plug of lamb's wool or cotton in the ears to keep them free of water while you continue the bath. Afterwards, check ears again to make sure they are dry.

Wash the face and head, using a wash cloth. Rinse and dry with a towel. Soak him all over now and pour shampoo on his back and shoulders, working up a good lather. Be sure to wash his belly, legs, feet, and tail, as well as his back and sides. A spray nozzle on a short hose is excellent for rinsing. The water should be comfortably warm.

Rub briskly with a turkish towel (it may take more than one); when he is completely dry, he may be combed. Never comb a wet Westie.

Westies love to work with their owners. They are easily trained to stand and *beg* since standing on the hind legs seems to be a natural instinct for the breed.

# TRAINING YOUR WESTIE

You owe proper training to your Westie. The right and privilege of being trained is his birthright; and whether your Westie is going to be a handsome, well-mannered housedog and companion, a show dog, or whatever possible use he may be put to, the basic training is always the same—all must start with basic obedience, or what might be called "manner training."

Your Westie must come instantly when called and obey the "Sit" or "Down" command just as fast; he must walk quietly at "Heel," whether on or off lead. He must be mannerly and polite wherever he goes; he must be polite to strangers on the street and in stores. He must be mannerly in the presence of other dogs. He must not bark at children on roller skates, motorcycles, or other domestic animals. And he must be restrained from chasing cats. It is not a dog's inalienable right to chase cats, and he must be reprimanded for it.

**Train your dog to fetch with a chicken-flavored Nylabone. Your Westie can smell it, you can't. They will retrieve the bone and bring it to you when called. Obviously retrieving follows COME training.**

## PROFESSIONAL TRAINING

How do you go about this training? Well, it's a very simple procedure, pretty well standardized by now. First, if you can afford the extra expense, you may send your Westie to a professional trainer, where in 30 to 60 days he will learn how to be a "good dog." If you enlist the services of a good professional trainer, follow his advice of when to come to see the dog. No, he won't forget you, but too-frequent visits at the wrong time may slow down his training progress. And using a "pro" trainer means that you will have to go for some training, too, after the trainer feels your Westie is ready to go home. You will have to learn how your Westie works, just what to expect of him and how to use what the dog has learned after he is home.

## OBEDIENCE TRAINING CLASS

Another way to train your Westie (many experienced Westie people think this is the best) is to join an obedience training class right in your own community. There is such a group in nearly every

It is impossible to train a Westie in a group...better just to have fun!

community nowadays. Here you will be working with a group of people who are also just starting out. You will actually be training your own dog, since all work is done under the direction of a head trainer who will make suggestions to you and also tell you when and how to correct your Westie's errors. Then, too, working with such a

Train your Westie to SIT on command. This is easy when you offer him a treat but refuse to give it until he sits down.

Frisbees® with the bone on top are the best for Westies. They find it difficult to pick up a Frisbee laying on the flat ground. Only use a Frisbee® made especially for dogs. Frisbees® made of cheap plastic are quickly chewed up and become dangerous.

SUCCESSFUL DOG TRAINING is one of the better books on dog training. The author, Michael Kamer, trains dogs for movie stars in Hollywood.

group, your Westie will learn to get along with other dogs. And, what is more important, he will learn to do exactly what he is told to do, no matter how much confusion there is around him or how great the temptation is to go his own way.

Write to your national kennel club for the location of a training club or class in your locality. Sign up. Go to it regularly—every session! Go early and leave late! Both you and your Westie will benefit tremendously.

This Westie holds the Nylabone® in place with his paws while he chews on the knobs. No dog bone has proven better than Nylabone® for controlling plaque on the Westie's teeth and giving him the relief of the doggie tension which makes all dogs chew.

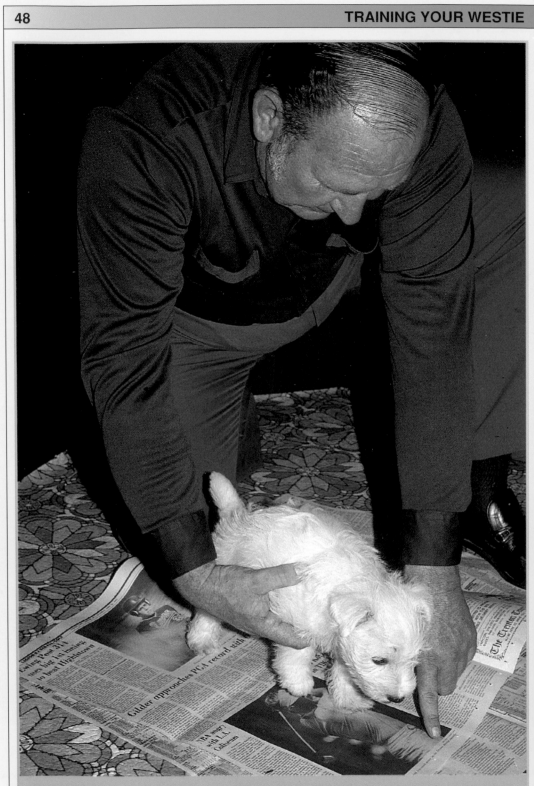

The most imperative training is house training. This begins with a piece of soiled newspaper. If you are serious about having a trained Westie, buy a dog training book and follow it page by page. A few months training will give you a 15-year benefit.

This Westie climbed from the couch to the table and is in danger of ruining some family heirlooms! Train your Westie not to climb onto tables.

## TRAIN HIM BY THE BOOK

The third way of training your Westie is by the book. Yes, you can do it this way and do a good job of it too. But in using the book method, select a book, buy it, study it carefully; then study it some more, until the procedures are almost second nature to you. Then start your training. But stay with the book and its advice and exercises. Don't start in and then make up a few rules of your own. If you don't follow the book, you'll get into jams you can't get out of by yourself. If after a few hours of short training sessions your Westie is still not working as he should, get back to the book for a study session, because it's your fault, not the dog's! The procedures of dog training have been so well systemized that it must be your fault, since literally thousands of fine Westies have been trained by the book.

After your Westie is "letter perfect" under all conditions, then, if you wish, go on to advanced training and trick work.

Your Westie will love his obedience training, and you'll burst with pride at the finished product! Your Westie will enjoy life even more, and you'll enjoy your Westie more. And remember—you *owe good training to your Westie.*

Retractable leashes are the preferred type for Westies and enable you to adjust the length of the leash. Photograph courtesy of Hagen.

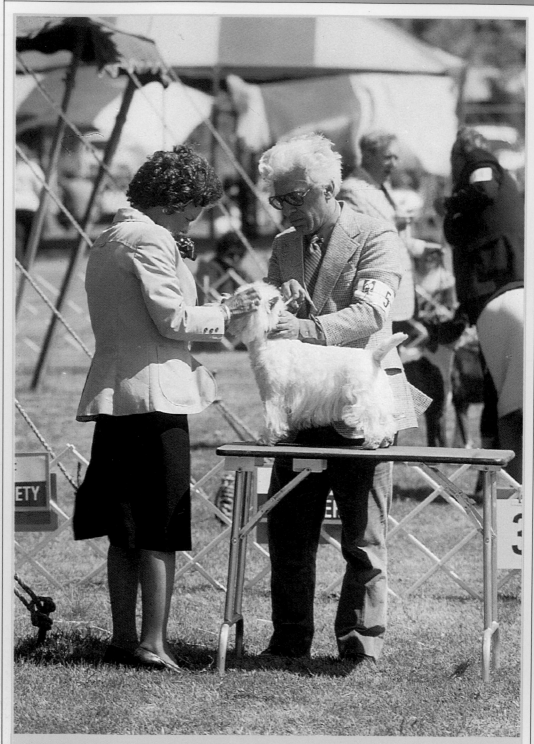

A Westie being examined by a judge at a dog show. Showing your Westie can be a lot of fun. You meet nice people with the same interests as you have. Attend a few shows, talk with the judges and the owners. See for yourself the pleasure of showing your Westie.

# SHOWING YOUR WESTIE

A show Westie is a comparatively rare thing. He is one out of several litters of puppies. He happens to be born with a degree of physical perfection that closely approximates the standard by which the breed is judged in the show ring. Such a dog should, on maturity, be able to win or approach his championship in good, fast company at the larger shows. Upon finishing his championship, he is apt to be as highly desirable as a breeding animal. As a proven stud, he will automatically command a high price for service.

This is a gorgeous dog, but it may never win the Westminster Show where only champions compete against each other.

Showing Westies is a lot of fun—yes, but it is a highly competitive sport. While all the experts were once beginners, the odds are against a novice. You will be showing against experienced handlers, often people who have devoted a lifetime to breeding, picking the right ones, and then showing those dogs through to their championships. Moreover, the most perfect Westie ever born has faults, and in your hands the faults will be far more evident than with the experienced handler who knows how to minimize his Westie's faults. These are but a few points on the sad side of the picture.

The experienced handler, as I say, was not born knowing the ropes. He learned—*and so can you!* You can if you will put in the same time, study and keen observation that he did. But it will take time!

## KEY TO SUCCESS

First, search for a truly fine show prospect. Take the puppy home, raise him by the book, and as carefully as you know how, give him every chance to mature into the Westie you hoped for. My advice is to keep your dog out of big shows, even Puppy Classes, until he is mature. Maturity in the male is roughly two years; with the female, 14 months or so. When your Westie is approaching maturity, start out at match shows, and, with this experience for both of you, then go gunning for the big wins at the big shows.

Next step, read the standard by which the Westie is judged. Study it until you know it by heart. Having done this, and while your puppy is at home (where he should be) growing into a normal, healthy Westie, go to every dog show you can possibly reach. Sit at the ringside and watch Westie judging. Keep your ears and eyes open. Do your own judging, holding each of those dogs against the standard, which you now know by heart.

In your evaluations, don't start looking for faults. Look for the virtues—the best qualities. How does a given Westie shape up against the standard? Having looked for and noted the virtues, then note the faults and see what prevents a given Westie from standing correctly or moving well. Weigh these faults against the virtues, since, ideally, every feature of the dog should contribute to the harmonious whole dog.

**A scene at a dog show where the Westie's gait is being observed by the judge.**

Scene at a dog show with the trainer preparing the Westie for the big event!

## "RINGSIDE JUDGING"

It's a good practice to make notes on each Westie, always holding the dog against the standard. In "ringside judging," forget your personal preference for this or that feature. What does the standard say about it? Watch carefully as the judge places the dogs in a given class. It is difficult from the ringside always to see why number one was placed over the second dog. Try to follow the judge's reasoning. Later try to talk with the judge after he is finished. Ask him questions as to why he placed certain Westies and not others. Listen while the judge explains his placings, and, I'll say right here, any judge worthy of his license should be able to give reasons.

When you're not at the ringside, talk with the fanciers and breeders who have Westies. Don't be afraid to ask opinions or say that you don't know. You have a lot of listening to do, and it will help you a great deal and speed up your personal progress if you are a good listener.

## THE NATIONAL CLUB

You will find it worthwhile to join the national Westie club and to subscribe to its magazine. From the national club, you will learn the location of an approved regional club near you. Now, when your young Westie is eight to ten months old, find out the dates of match shows in your section of the country. These differ from regular shows only in

When a really superb Westie develops, the showing is usually turned over to a professional trainer who takes the dog on the show circuit until it wins its championship. Puppies from a champion are worth a lot more than ordinary puppies.

**Set up your Westie to show off his best assets...and don't let his tail droop!**

that no championship points are given. These shows are especially designed to launch young dogs (and new handlers) on a show career.

**ENTER MATCH SHOWS**

With the ring deportment you have watched at big shows firmly in mind and practice, enter your Westie in as many match shows as you can. When in the ring, you have two jobs. One is to see to it that your Westie is always being seen to its best advantage. The other job is to keep your eye on the judge to see what he may want you to do next. Watch only the judge and your Westie. Be

quick and be alert; do exactly as the judge directs. Don't speak to him except to answer his questions. If he does something you don't like, don't say so. And don't irritate the judge (and everybody else) by constantly talking and fussing with your dog.

In moving about the ring, remember to keep clear of dogs beside you or in front of you. It is my advice to you *not* to show your Westie in a regular point show until he is at least close to maturity and after both you and your dog have had time to perfect ring manners and poise in the match shows.

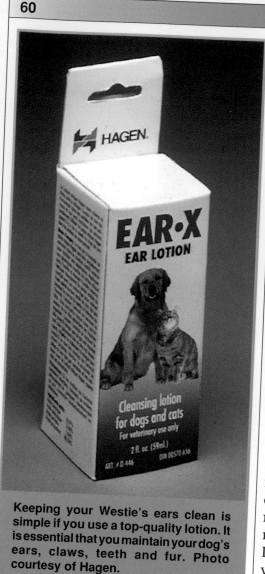

**Keeping your Westie's ears clean is simple if you use a top-quality lotion. It is essential that you maintain your dog's ears, claws, teeth and fur. Photo courtesy of Hagen.**

heavily treed areas, pastures or other outside grounds (such as dog shows or obedience or field trials). Athletic, active, and hunting dogs are the most likely subjects, though any passing dog can be the host. Remember Lyme disease is passed by tick infestation.

As for internal parasites, worms are potentially dangerous for dogs and people. Roundworms, hookworms, whipworms, tapeworms, and heartworms comprise the blightsome party of troublemakers. Deworming puppies begins at around two to three weeks and continues until three months of age. Proper hygienic care of the environment is also important to prevent contamination with roundworm and hookworm eggs. Heartworm preventatives are recommended by most veterinarians, although there are some drawbacks to the regular introduction of poisons into our dogs' system. These daily or monthly preparations also help regulate most other worms as well. Discuss worming procedures with your veterinarian.

Roundworms pose a great threat to dogs and people. They are found in the intestines of dogs, and can be passed to people through ingestion of feces-contaminated dirt. Roundworm infection can be prevented by not walking dogs in heavy-traffic people areas, by burning feces, and by curbing dogs in a responsible manner. (Of course, in most areas of the country, curbing dogs is the law.) Roundworms are typically passed from the bitch to the litter, and bitches should be treated along

inside. Discuss the possibilities with your vet. Not all products can be used in conjunction with one another, and some dogs may be more sensitive to certain applications than others. The dog's living quarters must be debugged as well as the dog itself. Heavy infestation may require multiple treatments.

Always check your dog for ticks well. Although fleas can be acquired almost anywhere, ticks are more likely to be picked up in with the puppies, even if she tested negative prior to whelping. Generally puppies are treated every two weeks until two months of age.

Hookworms, like roundworms, are also a danger to dogs and people. The hookworm parasite (known as *Ancylostoma caninum*) causes cutaneous larva migrans in people. The eggs of hookworms are passed in feces and become infective in shady, sandy areas. The larvae penetrate the skin of the dog, and the dog subsequently becomes infected. When swallowed, these parasites affect the intestines, lungs, windpipe, and the whole digestive system. Infected dogs suffer from anemia and lose large amounts of blood in the places where the worms latch onto the dog's intestines, etc.

Although infrequently passed to humans, whipworms are cited as one of the most common parasites in America. These elongated worms affect the intestines of the dog, where they latch on, and cause colic upset or diarrhea. Unless identified in stools passed, whipworms are difficult to diagnose. Adult worms can be eliminated more consistently than the larvae, since whipworms live unusual life cycles. Proper hygienic care of outdoor grounds is critical to the avoidance of these harmful parasites.

Tapeworms are carried by fleas, and enter the dog when the dog swallows the flea. Humans can acquire tapeworms in the same way, though we are less likely to swallow fleas than dogs are. Recent studies have shown that certain rodents and other wild animals have been infected with tapeworms, and dogs can be affected by catching and/or eating these other animals. Of course, outdoor hunting dogs and terriers are more likely to be infected in this way than are your typical house dog or non-motivated hound. Treatment for tapeworm has proven very effective, and infected dogs do not show great discomfort or symptoms. When people are infected, however, the liver can be seriously damaged. Proper cleanliness is the best bet against tapeworms.

Heartworm disease is transmitted by mosquitoes and badly affects the lungs, heart and blood vessels of dogs. The larvae of *Dirofilaria immitis* enter the dog's bloodstream when bitten by an infected mosquito. The larvae take about six months to mature.

Keep first aid cream on hand in case of cuts as it is antiseptic. Photo courtesy of Hagen.

The ideal pet is a Westie. Keep them healthy, well groomed, and well trained, and you can expect a dog's lifetime with you to be pure pleasure. He'll prove that a man's best friend is his dog!

The most complete book on the breed is THE BOOK OF THE WEST HIGHLAND WHITE TERRIER by Anna Katherine Nicholas. Your pet shop will have it. ISBN 0-86622-663-X.

The best book on dog's health is the OWNER'S GUIDE TO DOG HEALTH by Dr. Lowell Ackerman. Available at your local pet shop.

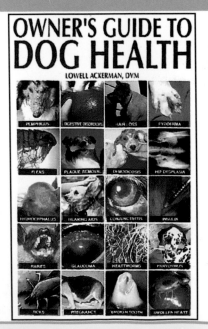

Treatment of heartworm disease has been effective but can be dangerous also. Prevention as always is the desirable alternative. Ivermectin is the active ingredient in most heartworm preventatives and has proven to be successful. Check with your veterinarian for the preparation best for your dog.

*The Publisher wishes to acknowledge the following owners of the dogs in this book for cooperating with our Photographers:*
*Chickie Anderson, Mitzi Beals, Janis C. Chapman, Chernok Kennels, Mark and Sally George, Mr. and Mrs. McMahon , McManis Kennels, Frederick Melville, Mr. and Mrs. Servin, Jasmine and Thomas Smith, Kathleen Spradleg, Timberlane Kennels, Mr. and Mrs. Charles A. Toth, and Charles and Lee Trudeau.*

Every year a full-color book is published with portraits of all the great champion dogs who win at the Westminster Kennel Club, including the West Highland White Terrier. The book is not expensive and is a MUST if you are interested in showing your Westie.

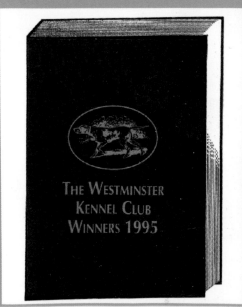